Praise for *Transce*

"*Transcendent Dreaming* takes its reader into a world where space and time are quite different than they are in waking life. Dr. Donnell's book provides remarkable evidence for the ability of dreams to inspire, to empower, and to heal."

—Stanley Krippner, Ph.D.
Coauthor of *Extraordinary Dreams and How to Work with Them*

"Christina Donnell's emphasis on the transcendent intelligence, the essence of Dreaming, creates a necessary and welcome basis for exploring dreams and everyday life. Her work is deep and easy to understand."

—Arny Mindell
Author of *Dreaming While Awake* and *Earth Based Psychology*

"When Christina Donnell, and others like her, share their transcendent experiences, the whole of humanity is rewarded. *Transcendent Dreaming* moves us that much closer to knowing more about who we are as a creation of an intelligent source. Now as we sleep, we can choose to awaken!"

—Tim Miejan
Managing editor, *Edge Life Magazine*

"*Transcendent Dreaming* is a revolutionary book. In clear, no-nonsense prose, Dr. Donnell recounts how, again and again over a period of several years, her dream states interlinked with and in some cases influenced the 'real' world. The implications of Dr. Donnell's work will be of interest to philosophers and physicists alike. And for the intrepid traveler on the path to higher consciousness, this book is an exciting new guide that goes even beyond the work of Carlos Castaneda."

—**Martha Lawrence, author of *Pisces Rising* and *Ashes of Aries***

"*Transcendent Dreaming* explores how dreams can transport us to the outer limits of human consciousness. From Dr. Donnell's rich and varied experience as a clinical psychologist, meditator, and serious student of shamanism, we learn about tools for transformation, healing, and even prophecy that can radically change how we view our lives. This important book delves into the miraculous while remaining grounded in real life experience."

—**Hal Zina Bennett, author of *The Lens of Perception***

"Who among us has not had a dream or vision that transcended what seems possible. This book will help us all tap into that hidden and uncontrollable part of us in which we find that occasionally our body and mind are not separate and time and space do not exist. For anyone who believes there is a vibrational shift now occurring, this book is a must read."

—Bill Manahan, M.D.
Past President, American Holistic Medical Association
Assistant Professor Emeritus, University of Minnesota
Medical School

"With cutting precision, Christina has eloquently nailed the description of the Void That Is Full. Finally someone has rhetorically pinned down this nebulous yet very real aspect of our vast reality."

—Mary Summer Rain, author of *In Your Dreams*

"Donnell has the ability to shatter all your previous perceptions of the concrete world, opening your mind and awakening your heart to your own boundless possibilities."

—Kaylin Richardson, 2006 Olympian, Alpine Skiing

"Dr. Donnell, likely because of her strong background in professional psychology and direct experience of indigenous shamanic teaching, is able to guide the reader along a bridge not only between the dreaming and waking worlds, but between ego identity and transcendent reality. In relating a series of dreams instrumental to her own awakening, she provides a framework by which an explorer in any tradition might come to better understand the journey *they* are on."

—Joseph A. Amara, co-owner of Magus Books, Ltd.

"Reading Donnell is not just an intellectual journey but a physical experience. More than words, this text transmits an energetic signature that will absolutely open and expand you."

—Mary Jo Peppler
International Volleyball Hall of Fame, Olympian

"Christina Donnell's dream and waking experiences make fascinating reading! Her ideas about the evolution of human consciousness, particularly in their relationship to dreaming, and the ability to remember dreams are most intriguing."

—Reverend Jeremy Taylor, D.Min.
Cofounder and past president of the International Association for the Study of Dreams and Executive Director of the Marin Institute for Projective Dream Work

Transcendent Dreaming

STEPPING INTO OUR HUMAN POTENTIAL

Christina Donnell, Ph.D.

FOREWORD BY LARRY DOSSEY, M.D.

WINDS OF CHANGE BOOKS
Minneapolis, Minnesota

Published by:
Winds of Change Books
1313 Fifth Street SE
Minneapolis, MN 55414

Editor: Ellen Kleiner
Book design and typography: Angela Werneke

Printed in Canada on 100% recycled paper

PUBLISHER'S CATALOGING-IN-PUBLICATION DATA

Donnell, Christina.

    Transcendent dreaming : stepping into our human potential / Christina Donnell. -- 1st ed. -- Minneapolis, Minn. : Winds of Change Books, c2008.

        p. ; cm.

        ISBN: 978-0-9801810-2-9
        Includes bibliographical references.

        1. Dreams. 2. Mind and body. 3. Self-actualization (Psychology) I. Title.

BF1091 .D66 2008   2007942414
135/.3--dc22   0809

10 9 8 7 6 5 4 3 2 1

You that give new life to this planet,

you that transcend logic,

come.

—JALALUDDIN RUMI

—— *ACKNOWLEDGMENTS* ——

I would like to express my gratitude to the following people:

My editor, Ellen Kleiner of Blessingway, for her remarkable vision and mastery and for her loving commitment to this book from conception to completion. I admire her refined talent immensely and her genuine dedication to bringing the work of her authors to the public.

Christina Dent, Louise Dollin, Deborah Goldberg, Beth Moore, Ciara O'Shea, Mary Jo Peppler, and Pat Shea, for their mindful reviews of the manuscript and invaluable recommendations.

Steve Moore, for our all-night conversation under the stars that led me to decide to publish this book.

Sheri Harris, for twenty-five years of spiritual camaraderie and her uncensored feedback while reviewing multiple versions of each chapter.

And Margaret Mills, for her friendship and support during the most arduous years of dreaming.

—— CONTENTS ——

FOREWORD *by Larry Dossey, M.D.* ✳ 11

PREFACE ✳ 15

INTRODUCTION: *The Dreaming* ✳ 21

DREAM I: *A Radical Shift in Consciousness* ✳ 31

DREAM II: *Crossing the Threshold of Ordinary Reality* ✳ 45

DREAM III: *Piercing the Illusion of Time and Space* ✳ 51

DREAM IV: *Merging with the Dreaming* ✳ 59

DREAM V: *Materialization and the Challenging of Conventional Reality* ✳ 67

DREAM VI: *Stepping Outside of Time* ✳ 77

DREAM VII: *Reconfiguring Energy* ✳ 85

DREAM VIII: *Dominion with Nature* ✳ 93

DREAM IX: *Cocreating with Awareness* ✳ 101

DREAM X: *Transcendent Living in a Linear World* ✳ 109

CONCLUSION: *The Transcendent Human* ✳ 117

NOTES ✳ 121

SUGGESTED READING ✳ 125

*C*hristina Donnell's *Transcendent Dreaming* is one of the most profound accounts of dreaming ever written by a westerner—destined, I believe, to take its place in the canon of dream literature.

For Donnell, dreaming became a nocturnal spiritual path that culminated in realizations described by the greatest mystics worldwide. These include the yielding of self or ego to an identification with a universal intelligence; transitioning from active doing to a state of being; relinquishing of a what's-it-good-for attitude in favor of an awareness of preexisting harmony and perfection; transcendence of linear time and rigid causality; a shift from intellectual, analytical reasoning to a humble acceptance of profound mystery; and a pervasive experience of wonder and joy.

Donnell's awareness did not arrive fully formed, however, but in concert with groundwork laid over the course of many years. She spent eighteen years practicing martial arts and Zen meditation, immersed herself in traditions of the indigenous Q'ero medicine people of South America, obtained a Ph.D. in clinical psychology and practiced her art for nearly two decades, and freely communicated her insights to others in seminars around the world.

My interest in Donnell's experiences stems from a life in medicine, which has included personal experiences that affirm her key insights. I've experienced precognitive dreams that have sometimes been eerily prophetic, and my patients have shared similar experiences with me. I've spent two decades focusing on healing research that shows that the compassionate, prayerful, loving intentions of a healer can generate healing influences at a distance, even though the recipient may be unaware they are being offered. Currently hundreds of studies reveal statistically significant results in both humans and nonhumans, including animals, plants, and even microbes. Like most physicians, I've seen radical cures unexplainable by conventional means seeming to occur as a blessing, a grace.

The primary significance of these findings and Donnell's insights is not that they constitute a therapeutic tool for the physician's black bag, although they can indeed be used to foster wholeness and healing. Their main importance is what they tell us about the nature of consciousness. They present us with a picture of the mind infinite in space and time — what I call *nonlocal* mind. The implications of nonlocal mind are profound, for if some aspect of our consciousness is infinite or nonlocal with respect to space, it is omnipresent, and if infinite or nonlocal with respect to time, then immortal or eternal. Nonlocal mind therefore affirms the existence of what has traditionally been called the soul. In the dimension she calls the Dreaming, Christina Donnell has experienced her nonlocal being as a living reality.

When first encountering the dream experiences Donnell describes—awakening the potential for prophecy, clairvoyance, stepping out of time, materialization, and more—many individuals are tempted to view them prag-matically. What are these insights *good* for? How can they be *used*? In fact, they *can* be used for practical purposes, but to limit one's view to utilitarian considerations vulgarizes such majestic visions, sometimes causing people to use the knowledge for manipulating and controlling others, a frequently recognized hazard on the spiritual path. Donnell, to her great credit, simply grew around and beyond this stumbling block.

Has the universe birthed Christina Donnell and this book because of an urgent need in a desperate time? One is tempted to think so. Amidst today's destruction of natural habitats and species, epidemics of old and new diseases, grinding poverty and widespread starvation, persistent genocides, religious fanaticism, and global terrorism, fear of "the other" is rampant, prompting nations to arm themselves to the teeth in preparation for God knows what. Donnell's vision reveals that this madness can be overcome. In the Dreaming, she has seen and participated in a oneness with all of creation. If we are to flourish as a species, the realization of this connectivity, this web of life, is crucial.

Donnell's testament leaves readers with questions: Might I have these experiences? Can I go where she has gone? The answer is yes. You are already there. You have only to realize it.

I bow deeply to Christina Donnell for showing the way.

Larry Dossey, M.D.

Author of *The Power of Premonitions* (forthcoming),

Healing Words, and *Recovering the Soul*

*F*or me, dreaming is an impulse within my soul. I came into this world as a proficient dreamer. When I was a little girl, I couldn't wait to go to bed at night because in my dreams I would fly with great skill, making it fun to constantly experience both new and familiar events. At age seven, I wrote my first book, a six-page treatise on African American spirituals. Given that I was being educated in a predominately white elementary school, my teacher and parents were perplexed about my choice of topic and wondered how I knew the lyrics to African American spirituals. I remember telling them that I had had a dream in which people singing spirituals had taught them to me.

Sometimes dreams entirely alter the course of a life. In December 1990, when I was twenty-eight, I had my first such experience, a prophetic dream in which I witnessed my father's final living moments and subsequent death. In the dream, it was a cold winter morning, and I saw my father's breath misting the air as he unloaded his grand-children's toys from the family car. I witnessed him surveying the forty-acre farm where he had raised his family, kissing my mother's side of the bed, and telling the family dog to protect the homestead. He then drove down to the local store, where he bought a Mountain Dew and told the owner to live every day fully. After getting back in the car, he pulled out an old family picture from his wallet, kissed it, and returned it to his wallet. Next he drove toward town but ended up on a country road. As the car acceler-ated, it veered off the road, hitting a large, old oak tree. With the impact, I was catapulted out of my body in the dream and entered a state of ecstatic union, coexisting with my father as pure awareness, both of us looking down at his lifeless body. In that state, we had an exchange that made me see there is no distinction between death and the divine. Finally, I became vaguely aware of my body and awoke from the dream.

At the time of the dream, my father was ill with Lou Gehrig's disease, or ALS, and had been given less than six months to live. Although I could not explain the expe-rience of becoming pure awareness and coexisting with my father in an ecstatic state, I assumed the dream had occurred because my psyche was preparing me for his impending death. The morning following the dream, I reported as usual to my job as director of the anxiety disorders clinic in the Department of Psychiatry at St. Paul Ramsey Medical Center. Midmorning a colleague came to my office and informed me that my father had been killed in a car accident.

The next day, when I arrived at my childhood home in Michigan for the funeral, the usual events that surround a death were underway. I said nothing about my dream, even though my younger brother asked if I would like him to comment on the viewing of our father's body before it had been cremated and I replied, "No, but his jaw was really messed up wasn't it?" Without questioning how I could know this information, he answered, "Yeah, I think you will be glad you didn't view the body."

After the funeral, talk turned toward the possibility that my father had taken his own life, which again made me wonder about the prophetic nature of the dream. Finally, my father's personal effects were given to my mother and, from my father's wallet, she took out the exact family photo I had watched him kiss in the dream. Initially, I was just unnerved by these coincidences between my dream and reality. But the shock of witnessing gradually more manifestations of the dream's precise details eventually forced me to confront possibilities of increased awareness through dreams I never could have imagined before, including prophecy and the experience of consciousness without boundaries.

After experiencing that dream and subsequent events, I knew three things: the dream was prophetic; I had accessed another dimension of reality; and there is broader, more profound knowledge available in dreams than is offered through everyday reality. What I did not know was how I had had the dream. I was also unaware that it was only the first of many such dream experiences, and that my life from this point on would take a markedly different direction.

Following the prophetic dream about my father's passing, I resigned from my position at the clinic, opened a private practice, and traveled to indigenous cultures to investigate shamanic perspectives. I also continued my training in Zen meditation and Shotakan Karate, both of which I had started shortly before my father's death.

Then in 1996 I had another pivotal dream that radically shifted my consciousness. The dream, about a mesmerizing black jaguar, described in the first chapter of this book, confirmed for me that I was gradually awakening to the true source of my being and the limitless potential inherent within each of us as human beings.

Because the kind of dreaming I was experiencing differed from any I had known or read about, I hesitated for many years to write about the episodes, doubting whether they would be accepted as truthful accounts. Yet as dream after dream unfolded, I became aware that embedded in such experiences was a blueprint for a transcendent humanity that could contribute to the awakening of our infinite human potential.

I was familiar with Carlos Castaneda's ground-breaking work on dreaming, and had likewise experienced the dreamer as an intermediary between the everyday world and an unseen world. But while in Castaneda's writings the experience of the dreamer was often adversarial or predatory, and therefore suggestive of separation, the dreams I was having evoked instead a distinct communion with energy behind the visible world. This departure from Castaneda's view most likely originated in two overlapping traditions that had taken root within me: the long custom in Asian literature of exploring ways to achieve oneness and in the Americas of using dreams to enrich human perceptions.

It eventually became clear that my personal history—eighteen years of martial arts practice and Zen meditation, sixteen years of shamanic training, and education as a clinical psychologist—provided the framework for the unfolding of what I now call "transcendent dreaming." I use the word *transcendent* to emphasize the shift my journey underwent from identification with the individual self to identification with our true, limitless nature connected with the divine intelligence that animates the universe.

Transcendent Dreaming is for the many people now awakening to their latent human potential. In a way, this book attempts the impossible—to describe states beyond reason and language. I hope that by sharing my own dream experiences, I will help increase readers' awareness of the untapped potential within them. At the very least, may it convey the promise inherent in a life lived from the true source of our being: the blossoming of inner peace, wholeness, and joy not dependent on external conditions, and the wonderment of merging with the Creator of all things.

The Dreaming

*D*reaming is not just having dreams, daydreaming, or imagining. Dreaming opens up other realms and involves both bodily processes and levels of mental awareness. Through dreaming we perceive and participate in realities we can describe, even though we can't explain what makes us perceive them. In dreaming, whether during sleep or while awake, you undergo an energetic shift in which your ordinary identity relaxes and an all-encompassing, formless you emerges to interact with the greater invisible field in which you are living. In transcendent dreaming, you participate in the divine intelligence that animates the universe.

There are three basic levels of dreaming, each with its own rewards. In ordinary dreaming, the dreamer is primarily a passive participant witnessing the form of a dream. Ordinary dreaming can be a valuable source of practical insights about significant life situations, such as personal conflicts, relationships with others, or one's life purpose.

This level of dreaming may bring understanding and support for personal transformation that can have healing applications.

Another level of dreaming is lucid dreaming. This occurs when a person is able to awaken within a dream, maintain awareness of dreaming, and often control the course of the dream. Lucid dreams are also much more vivid than ordinary dreams. As a dreamer becomes proficient in lucid dreaming, other capacities open up, such as the ability to experience consciousness in more than one place at a time, to interpenetrate matter, and to coexist in the same place with bodies of a similar material.

Transcendent dreaming has all the qualities of ordinary and lucid dreaming yet offers more. In transcendent dreaming the dreamer has waking consciousness while merging beyond the form of the dream into its source. The source of the dream is the same intelligence that guides creation. When we awaken within this source, we become one with it and our infinite nature emerges. In this way, transcendent dreaming serves as a bridge between manifest and nonmanifest reality.

The thirteenth-century Persian mystic poet known to Westerners simply as Rumi wrote of a continuous essence moving through form; like the sun, its presence is sometimes palpable, sometimes not, but it is always there.[1] Similarly, the intelligence that guides creation is sometimes palpable, sometimes not, and yet always there, generating life force. Awakening within it through transcendent dreaming provides an opportunity to both witness creation and participate consciously in it. In this sense, transcendent dreaming involves both a surrendering and a radical shift in consciousness. As a form of cocreating, it offers, above all, a way to fall deeply in love with creation.

One of the challenges in preparing for transcendent dreaming is to comprehend the concept of different but simultaneous realities—the tangible reality of everyday life and the more primary level of reality that gives birth to all the objects and appearances of the manifest world. The idea of two realities can be found in almost all spiritual traditions. Tibetan Buddhists call them the void and the nonvoid; all things in the universe pour out of the void in a boundless flux and into the nonvoid, the realm of visible objects.[2] Hindus call the deeper level of reality Brahman. Brahman is formless and the source of all forms, which appear out of it and resolve back into it endlessly.[3] The Dogon people of the western Sudan likewise believe that the physical world is perpetually flowing out of and streaming back into a more fundamental level of reality.[4] Taoists call the primary level of reality "the Tao that cannot be spoken," while Native Americans refer to it as the power of the Great Spirit. Aboriginal Australians believe that the true source of the mind is in the transcendent reality, or what they call the Dreamtime.[5] Similarly, central to shamanic traditions around the world is the notion that underlying all visible forms, both animate and inanimate, is a vital essence from which they emerge and by which they are nurtured.

More recently, quantum physicists such as David Bohm have called the deeper, more primary level of reality the implicate, or enfolded, order and refer to our everyday world as the explicate, or unfolded, order. Bohm and many of his colleagues believe that our consciousness has its source in the implicate order of reality.[6] The fact that many artists, mystics, and poets throughout history have developed the ability to tap into the wisdom bubbling up from a deeper level of existence indicates that our consciousness may indeed be sourced in the implicate level of reality.

I call this deeper level of reality, this creative intelligence behind and within creation, the Dreaming. It is the life force of all living things—galaxies, human beings, and trees—as well as the power in corporations and communities. While an ordinary dream is a fleeting play of forms reflecting the world in a somewhat but not entirely real way, the Dreaming, the reality from which the forms come and to which they return, is the absolute behind the relative, the timeless behind the temporal, the substratum that makes the dream possible. The Dreaming, or consciousness itself, is also synonymous with the sunlike essence that can be perceived and experienced through transcendent dreaming.

Transcendent dreaming differs in other ways as well from ordinary and lucid dreaming. When you awaken within a lucid dream, you still have a feeling of separation. You are observing the dream. By contrast, when you awaken within a transcendent dream, you merge into the dream experience and, ultimately, into the substratum from which the dream is occurring, which is the Dreaming. When you merge into this energy that created the form of the dream, you feel no separation. The "I" is dissolved into the One. There is no observer or observation, only observing.

Further, in an ordinary dream, you may dream of a

rose. In a lucid dream, you may awaken within the dream, see the rose, and watch yourself smell the rose and experience its fragrance. In a transcendent dream, you awaken within the dream, see the rose, and merge into it. There is no you, no fragrance, and no experience of fragrance. You have become the fragrance. At this level of experience, there is no doing, only being and the experience of transcendent reality and our infinite nature.

In his book *Mastery of Love*, Miguel Ruiz describes the resulting transcendent awareness as the discovery that you are a force making it possible for your body to live and your mind to dream. The whole universe, he tells us, is a living being moved by this force.[7] Similarly, in a transcendent dream you know that you are not your body or your mind, yet you are aware as never before that you exist. You know yourself as consciousness. Once you find this out, not by logic but by experience, you also discover that you are one with the force that organizes sunflowers and galaxies, that moves the wind and breathes through the body.

Transcendent dreaming allows you to experience a connection with this immeasurable, indestructible force that is paradoxically you and yet much greater than you. When you ultimately merge into the Dreaming, the boundary between consciousness and matter dissolves, and you are awakened to a new state of existence. From this point of view, to speak of consciousness and matter as interacting has no meaning. The observer *is* the observed—they are the same, except they exist in different states. It is through this participatory exchange that you awaken to the true source of your being and the limitless power inherent within you.

Throughout history many great mystics, prophets, and men and women of genius have come in direct contact with the Dreaming and have demonstrated the materialization and power that derive from living in connection with this force birthing creation. For example, Jesus was a perfect embodiment of this potential, demonstrated by his ability to spontaneously heal others, calm the weather, and reappear in a new body, resurrected with a continuation of consciousness. He revealed that through love of what he called God—what I call the Dreaming—and love of the other as self, we could be radically transformed and do the work he did.

Padre Pio, the famous Italian priest, never left the San Giovanni Monastery where he lived yet was seen dressing the wounds of soldiers on the battlefield during World War

II and even at the Vatican conferring with the pope. American fighter pilots flying in the vicinity of San Giovanni Rotundo later recounted how they had been unable to bomb the area after spotting the figure of a monk, at times a towering apparition in the clouds.[8]

Perhaps the most famous modern-day materializations are those produced by Sathya Sai Baba, a holy man from south India. Numerous witnesses have reported watching Sai Baba snap his fingers and vanish, instantly reappearing a hundred or more yards away. Sai Baba practices materialization in this way to administer to others. He is especially known for his ability to produce an endless supply of *vibhuti,* or sacred ash, from his hands.[9] These are only a few of the many historical figures who have demonstrated the unlimited human potential that is the birthright of every human being.

For most people such an awakening does not occur as a single, transformative event but as a gradual unfolding. For those few individuals who experience a sudden, dramatic awakening, there is nevertheless a graduated evolution as the new consciousness becomes integrated into our lives. Whether it happens incrementally or constitutes a quantum leap in consciousness, transcendent dreaming awakens the transcendent abilities that lie dormant in human beings and are the natural heritage of the human race.

This book chronicles one woman's experience of awakening latent human potential through dreaming. The chapters focus on ten of my dreams that best illustrate the process of awakening to our transcendent nature. They are organized and sequenced in a way that allows the reader to witness the dream experiences as they unfold and learn increasingly more about their significance for expanding consciousness and accessing transcendent reality. I have thus replicated for the reader the gradual unfolding of my awakening, from my disorientation that followed the first dream, to my growing ability to integrate these experiences. In cases where the dreams materialized and impacted specific people's lives, their names have been changed and some circumstances slightly altered to protect the identities of individuals involved.

The first two dream experiences recount an initial radical transformation in my consciousness. The third dream reveals how connected we all are and what can happen when our consciousness transcends space. The fourth dream emphasizes the impact of subtle realms of reality on the manifest world. Dreams five and six show the profound changes in perception that occur upon merging into the source of the dreams, what I call the Dreaming. While the seventh dream marks a new level of perception from a point of consciousness outside the body, the eighth dream integrates the preceding dream experiences. The final two dreams reflect cocreation and engagement with a linear world from a multidimensional reality. The account of each dream experience is followed by reflections on its meaning and significance for developing our transcendent nature.

Ultimately, this book reveals a path by which we can access our infinite nature and contains a blueprint for a transcendent humanity. Included as well are thoughts on how to live in the ordinary world after accessing that transcendent reality. Awakening to the true source of our being and experiencing the Dreaming inherent within us enlivens perceptions and capacities beyond any we know in our everyday world, making the possibilities limitless.

When we know ourselves as one with the Dreaming, there is no earth or heaven—all is the Dreaming. From that moment on, perpetual joy, knowledge, and love become a way of life.

—— *DREAM I* ——

A Radical Shift in Consciousness

*M*y first nonprophetic dream that revealed to me the radical shift in consciousness possible through dreaming contained imagery that emerged from my experiences with Zen meditation and shamanic trainings. At the time, I maintained a private practice as a clinical psychologist and taught workshops on shamanism between my own shamanic trainings and world travels.

For the previous six years I had been instructed in Zen meditation by a sensei (teacher) who explained that the mind is structured in layers, as is the universe, from the superficial to the profound. When we use the mind at the superficial level of ordinary thought, she said, our power is limited. But when we use the mind to access deeper levels of consciousness,

31

a different kind of power becomes available. Consciousness at the deepest levels of the mind is capable of creating universes. Then she added, "You must quiet the mind to know these deeper levels of consciousness. You must develop singleness of mind so the energy density of your mind becomes greater and you can know a different kind of power."

During that session, image after image had Rolodexed through my mind. I saw faces, the wiry hair on the underbelly of a dog, and various landscapes. Each image seemed alive and real, and I began to feel like I had as a child flying in my dreams. When I asked her if this was normal, she shook her head no and said, "The images are distractions. Your mind is not still. This is why you need to meditate."

Such images never ceased spinning through my mind and were usually so vivid they inevitably held my attention. One mesmerizing image that appeared repeatedly was a black jaguar sitting in a tree surveying a jungle below. After seeing it three times, I began wondering why the jaguar was always in the tree watching the world with detachment. Eventually I realized that it was an apt metaphor for that period of my life: I had left an eleven-year relationship, terminated my adjunct faculty position at the University of Minnesota, resigned from my position as director of the anxiety disorders clinic at the medical center, and reduced my martial arts practice to a daily set of primary Qi Gong exercises working with the elements in nature. I had opted to shift from a life of ambition and activity to a more simple, qualitative, and reflective life in order to spend more time visiting and studying indigenous cultures and exploring my inner capabilities.

The following dream occurred in 1996. By then, although my familiar focus on ambition and activity in the external world had been replaced by exploration of my internal world, I was not yet comfortable with this transformation and had not yet integrated my inner discoveries with the everyday, repetitive events of my life. The dream seemed to reflect an intent to more deeply explore my internal world.

While I lay in bed with my eyes closed and my awareness centered between them, image after image appeared in my mind's eye. Meditation had accustomed me to letting images rise and evaporate without breaking my concentration. Then a heavy, syrupy feeling, which I eventually learned to associate with transcendent dreaming, blanketed me, pulling me into sleep.

I awakened within a dream in which I was doing exactly what I had been doing before the dream—lying in bed with my awareness centered between my eyes. Then the image of the black jaguar sitting in its tree, intently watching the jungle below, appeared and distracted me. The part of my awareness that was watching the dream thought it was peculiar that the jaguar image had appeared in a dream. With this thought, my awareness was drawn into the dream and became so immersed in the image of the jaguar that I lost sensation of my body and felt suspended in midair.

Although the sense of losing awareness of one's body and physical surroundings happens to many people who practice meditation, this was not meditation. In fact, I soon felt my awareness itself begin to dissolve. The sensation was so extraordinary and pleasing that my attention was irresistibly drawn further into the jaguar image. Suddenly, a piercing brilliant light, accompanied by extreme heat, entered my brain. Unprepared for such an experience, I became anxious and aware of my body again. As the illumination from inside of me grew brighter and brighter, I experienced a rocking sensation and then felt the point of consciousness that was myself gradually expanding beyond my body.

Meanwhile, my body had been dissolving until I became unconscious of it. I was now all consciousness—

without form, feeling, or sensation—spread out in every direction without limitation. I was no longer as I had always known myself to be, a small point of awareness confined in a body, but instead an infinite consciousness bathed in light and reveling in a state of exaltation.

After some time, I felt my consciousness contract, becoming smaller and smaller until I again was vaguely aware of the outline of my body. I spent some time wondering if I was going to slip back into my body but did not know how to do this. Eventually, it just happened, and I awakened from the dream, once more aware of my body and the cars passing on the street outside my window.

I felt dazed and bewildered, as if returning from a foreign land, but was soothed by the sun shining on my face through the window. My friend Miriam was sitting on the edge of my bed. I tried to lift my arms and hands, but they felt limp and lifeless. And while I could understand every word Miriam spoke, I could not sequence a thought or speak. I learned that I had been in this state for almost thirty-six hours. I had missed a full day of work and a dinner engagement with her, and when I did not answer the phone in the morning, she had come to check on me.

Eventually I stood up, although my legs felt weak and

wobbled beneath me. After a while, exhausted and ill at ease, I went outside for a short walk, thinking it would help me return to normalcy. I soon doubled up from an unbearable heat in my abdomen that rose to my throat, and I felt as if I would vomit fire. I returned to the house and sat on the couch, taking no interest in anything and feeling detached from my surroundings. Miriam spent the day to make sure I was okay, and left in the evening. Retiring early, I slept fitfully, having strange dreams yet aware that a part of myself was watching me sleep.

Around 5:00 a.m., the same heavy, syrupy feeling descended upon me again, and I awakened in the same dream as the night before. The jaguar was sitting in the same tree, intently watching the jungle below. Again I was pulled into the image, and light pierced my head, filling me with rapture and vitality. As I felt myself dissolve, my consciousness once again expanded in all directions then slowly contracted. When I finally became aware of my body, my heart was racing, there was a metallic taste in my mouth, and my exhaustion was even more pronounced than after the first dream.

I did not feel like the same woman I had been only a few days before. Something intangible and powerful, which

I could not grasp or analyze, was happening, and I could not free myself from a sense of apprehension. From that day forward, I would never be my old self again. For the next several years I would live suspended between spirit and matter, between heaven and earth.

Reflections

The days immediately following the dream were a prolonged nightmare. I was aware of an intense internal glow, always in rapid motion. The nights were especially difficult since the stream of light that had pierced my head in both dreams seemed to increase in speed and intensity during the hours of darkness. I could feel my energy increasing, decreasing, and repatterning. I could distinctly feel and perceive the luminosity emanating into a field surrounding and connected to my body and habitually lay awake all night watching myself sleep or dream. With the increased energy coursing through my body, my arms and hands seemed to take on a life of their own. When I was lying, my body would vibrate, regardless of the surface it was on. Images rapidly Rolodexed through my mind's eye. When one became fixed, I was gripped with fear because I had no control over being pulled into it and having my awareness consequently dissolve. Soon the images began to occur even with my eyes open, seemingly a solvent working on the glue that held my awareness together.

Even more alarming was the fact that my consciousness was not as stable as it had been before but now expanded and contracted, regulated in a mysterious way by the images, making me fearful that a fine line now separated me from insanity. The expansion and contraction of my consciousness altered the way my mind functioned. I perceived a luminous glow around objects both in my mind's eye and in the physical environment. This glow never remained constant in dimension or intensity, but rather waxed and waned, and sometimes changed color.

Gopi Krishna, author and renowned twentieth-century yogi and teacher from India, noted a similar perception in response to first experiencing the awakening of kundalini,[1] but for me it went further. When the glow increased in size or brilliance, the urge to merge into it grew stronger, until my awareness dissolved into the unseen energies behind the manifest world. It was during this time that I began to have experiences of simultaneously lying in bed and walking around downstairs, with my awareness in both places. Three people—two friends and one client—independently told me they had awakened from sleep and seen me standing at the foot of their bed. I remembered lying in bed and simultaneously standing at the foot of one friend's bed, wondering what I was doing there, while I had no conscious recollection of the other incidents. I knew these experiences had something to do with the amount of energy coursing through my system and my merging with images.

By March 1997, all these experiences had taken their toll on my body. I suffered from extreme fatigue and simultaneously experienced a weird feeling of exaltation and melancholy. For a long time I remained uncertain about the meaning of my condition. From the point of view of my Zen meditation practice, I surmised that I had turned from witnessing the rise and fall of awareness to participating with objects or images in my field of awareness. The amount of energy concentrated in an image, the merging into a participatory exchange with it, and the energy from which the image itself had risen had shifted my perception. My perception had also become rooted in the sensual dimension of experience, born of the body's natural capacity to resonate with other forms; David Abram, in his work with traditional sorcerers, or *dukuns,* of the Indonesian archipelago, noted a similar anchoring of perception in sensual realities.[2] Thus what was considered a distraction in my Zen meditation practice had become a new way for me to engage with the sentient world.

From the point of view of my shamanic training, the dream seemed linked to my encounters with the traditions of Q'ero medicine people of the high Andes of Peru and transmissions associated with them. The Q'ero Indians are considered masters of the energy realm, which is the primary reality in which they live, and they communicate with nature through energy forces. For instance, they determine where they are in a large geographic area by the energetic feel of the terrain rather than by physical markers. For the Q'ero medicine people, every element of the landscape speaks: any movement may be purposeful, any sound meaningful. The more time I spent with the Q'ero, the more it became second nature to participate in discourse with animate nature and feel my body's inherent capacity to resonate with the landscape. Furthermore, the Q'ero do not live in linear time, and therefore do not acknowledge an event that just happened or will be occurring. Given that they related to me energetically, did not talk about what they were doing, and spoke Quechua, which had to be translated into Spanish and then English, I received most of their transmissions without the benefit of verbal delivery. While struggling to decipher the Q'ero, I began to see and hear in a manner I never had before.

Two months before the dream, I had received an energetic transmission called the *mosoq karpay* from don Manuel Quispe, the master medicine man of the Q'ero. Every time I received a transmission from him, I experienced for a day or two the same heavy, syrupy state as in the dream. Having this sensation in the dream and seeing the image of the black jaguar, which is highly revered in the Andes, suggested that my dream experience was related to the *mosoq karpay* transmission.

At the time of this dream, I knew there was evidence for the presence of forces and planes of existence other than those we perceive with our senses. I also realized that when other levels of reality are encountered, they revise the picture of the universe presented by the intellect. But I had no knowledge of the technicalities and implications of encountering different levels of reality other than through my dreaming experiences.

Today, after sixteen years of working with the Q'ero

medicine people, I better understand their means of perceiving various levels of reality and their techniques for preserving and transmitting knowledge. Whereas we customarily perceive an object or being, separate our awareness, and label it, the Q'ero merge into an object or being to experience it. They are masterful at entering into a participatory exchange with both seen and unseen sentient forms and forces. For instance, while they are unaware that water breaks down to one oxygen to two hydrogen atoms, they can easily call in the rain by merging with the energy behind and within the rain.

Because of my exposure to the Q'ero medicine people, I became increasingly adept at merging my awareness with nonhuman forms to gain direct understanding of them apart from my intellect. For example, by merging my awareness with plants I could learn what they were best used for and events that had occurred in their immediate environment. I had no idea that developing the ability to merge your own perception with another awareness could affect the mind and body so deeply. I am sure that merging my awareness with other forms also deepened my dreaming.

Although I lacked a theoretical framework for understanding these phenomena, they made me acutely aware of the existence of different levels of reality. I realized how we live in at least two worlds within the physical body alone. There is a macroscopic world that we see—our flesh and bones. And there is also a microscopic world of our life force: numberless subatomic fields where matter disappears and only probabilities exist, in a vacuum, somehow resulting in an exquisite balance within the body. These two domains are distinct yet complementary. Both are true; they are simply different levels of reality.

I now realized more than ever before that I was not only my flesh and bones but also countless fields of subatomic particles. Although I did not consciously know the mathematics involved at each level of reality, I felt as if I was in a participatory exchange with both. Physical, biochemical, and energetic shifts all seemed to be part of this new way of perceiving. The doorway to an expanded consciousness seemed to lead right back to my own body and mind—their quantum nature and limitless potential. What remained outside my understanding were my uncontrollable urges to enter images, resulting in the dissolution of my awareness. Not until much later did I realize this was the first stage of merging into the Dreaming, the invisible implicate level of reality that is the source of creation.

The alteration of my consciousness was evidence of this awakening. From a consciousness dominated by my ego and by socialization, it had expanded into a consciousness beyond anything familiar. My ego, or "I," remained, but instead of being a limited unit it was now a luminous field of vast dimensions. Ego consciousness and an infinitely extended field of awareness existed side by side, distinct from each other and yet one. It was as if my mind were both here and spread throughout time and space.

DREAM II

Crossing the Threshold of Ordinary Reality

For weeks after the first dream, my physical condition con-
tinued to deteriorate, and my consciousness was yet far from
steady. Any sustained effort at concentration invariably
intensified the experience of expanded consciousness until I
was all consciousness, everywhere at once, without form. In the
following dream, which occurred within two months of the first
one, I was confronted with the boundary between the realms of
life and death.

I awakened within a dream, witnessing the familiar energy
coursing through my body, alternately accelerating and
decelerating repeatedly. One last crescendo occurred, and
when it subsided I found myself being held in abeyance at

the threshold where we cross over to death. I was acutely aware of being shown how to die and what happens to awareness at that time. While in this suspended state, I could feel tension in every cell of my body yet also an infusion of bliss. After an unknown period of time, my mind and body grew fatigued, and the urge to cross over became strong. As more time passed, I simply surrendered, at which point my awareness dissolved until I became consciousness without form or limitation, and entered a state of ecstasy.

Twelve hours later I awakened with the same lassitude and inability to organize thoughts as after my first dream, two months before. Within hours, I came down with pneumonia.

Moreover, due to the dream's duration I had missed attending a Ph.D. student's dissertation defense, but nothing in the everyday world mattered to me. For several months I remained indifferent to being on the earth, longing for the other side without understanding why. Although the longing's precise purpose still eluded me, my dreaming had become a rigorous yet illuminating experience giving me insight into the different states of life and death and showing me my own and humanity's potential.

Reflections

This dream experience occurred repeatedly, in shorter durations. I knew I was encountering a multidimensional reality with levels of existence that differ in density. As with the first dream, this one left my mind unstable. My consciousness would often expand and contract uncontrollably, leaving me with energy coursing in and around my body. At times, when I closed my eyes, I could distinctly see the microscopic life-force fields of the body: innumerable circling currents, at some places creating vortices, all of them part of a vast sea of light, perpetually in motion, in and beyond my body. With the second dream, the new kind of activity developing within my body had further shifted my perception from observing to having a direct participatory exchange with the object of perception, whether it was a thought, image, or event.

As a by-product of the dream's recurrences, I soon became a midwife for those who were crossing over into the spirit realm. Finding myself at the side of animals and people who were dying, I was naturally able to accompany them on this journey. I was also able to assist people in coma states. But despite my willingness to work with these individuals, I felt indifferent to their condition—indeed, to life in general. I had loved my family, friends, and community from the depths of my being, but now I seemed to have no love for anything. I viewed this loss of affection with despondency, feeling robbed of that which gives life its greatest charm. Perceiving no sign of spiritual inspiration through these experiences, I had misgivings about what was happening to me.

I wanted to set my doubts to rest by finding some explanation for my condition, as well as a method to deal with it. Although my Q'ero shamanic teachers might have understood my condition, the language barrier prevented me from asking for an explanation. Without a teacher's wisdom to draw upon, I finally concluded that my expanded consciousness was in contact with the world of living energy. I realized that while energy is not normally perceptible to ordinary individuals, I might be experiencing the first subtle field to come within range of perception when consciousness expands. Apparently some latent capacity was unfolding within me, and it had an organic timing and life of its own; a participatory exchange with living energy had become my mentor, and dreaming was the medium for our relationship. Once I arrived at this conclusion, I threw my doubting to the wind and let my experiences unfold.

Over the next decade, my awareness in dreams and outside of them continued to merge into images, further redefining my perception and deepening my awareness of the Dreaming itself—the energy within and behind the images or dreams. My dreams seemed, increasingly, to be preparation for merging into the Dreaming, resulting in transcendent dreaming as a catalyst for awakening my limitless nature.

—— DREAM III ——

Piercing the Illusion of Time and Space

As my dream experiences became more common, I felt increasingly assured that I was in no imminent physical or mental danger. Although my body and mind were still somewhat unstable due to the constant fluctuations in my consciousness, my overall strength gradually increased. Ever since the initial dream experience, in which a fundamental shift in consciousness occurred, I did not require much sleep. When I did sleep, it was not restful because a part of me was watching myself sleep. The following dream made me more aware of how time and space are illusionary on other levels of reality.

I had gone to bed relaxed. Around two o'clock in the morning, the telltale heavy, syrupy sensation came over me. As it did, I felt the energy in my body alternately accelerating and decelerating with rapidity.

As the energy pattern slowed, I suddenly found myself as pure consciousness without form following a young boy with polio, who was singing while walking home from school, one brace on his leg, another held in his arms. I witnessed him eating dinner then clearing the dishes off the table. When it was time for him to get ready for bed, I watched his father accompany him to the bathroom, help him brush his teeth, take his leg braces off, and lovingly undress and help him into his pajamas. Then the father unzipped his own pants, pulled his penis out, and, taking the boy's hand in his, placed it on his penis. At that point, my consciousness began to merge with the boy, and I simultaneously became both his fear and excitement, as well as a formless energy that was shifting him in some way.

When he was safely in bed, I became aware that if I left the dream I would no longer be the boy's guardian, which caused great conflict within me. I knew I could stay in this state indefinitely or return to my body, although I couldn't remember why I would want to return to my body since I was completely disconnected from it. After suddenly becoming a pattern of energy that rapidly accelerated then decelerated, with great sadness I chose to return to my own body.

The most interesting part of this dream experience unfolded five years later. I was having dinner one evening with a man I had known since my early twenties. We talked about his father's imminent death, and he asked if I could suggest a good therapist so he could work out some childhood issues to get closure on his relationship with his father before he died. I suggested a therapist he might like working with. As we were getting ready to leave the restaurant, he slid out of the booth, heavily adjusted his weight, and said, "This leg gives me some problems every now and then. I had polio as a child."

I felt like I had been struck by a lightning bolt, suddenly realizing that he was the boy in my dream experience five years earlier. I was left to ponder the ways in which we are all connected and how, on other levels of reality experienced in dreams, our sense of time and space can dissolve, underscoring their illusionary quality.

Reflections

This dream was one of many in which I became a shape-less mass of energy that merged into an image. Sometimes this energy first organizes itself into a form, other times not, but either way it inevitably merges with a form in the dream. When this happens, I experience both the energy and the feeling state of the form into which it has merged. Action occurs through me, and often the energy provides assistance in some way.

Although in most cases I have not had contact later with the participants in the dream, such contact has occasionally occurred. In one instance, I was having lunch with a colleague who said offhandedly, "I have a friend who may be interested in taking one of the shamanic workshops you teach. I am not sure she would be appropriate since she had an experience that resulted in her becoming a funda-mentalist Christian."

I innocently asked her what the experience was, always curious about events that transform people's lives.

My colleague said, "Several years ago my friend was in a terrible motorcycle accident in which her boyfriend was significantly injured. As if in slow motion, she felt a pair of hands cradle her head, which was helmetless, guide it as the motorcycle skidded and she tumbled onto the pavement, and remain there until the emergency vehicles arrived."

Underneath my calm exterior, I was rendered speechless. I had had a dream experience seven years earlier in which the identical action had occurred, with my hands cradling the woman's head and my awareness, having become the woman's hands, dissolving as I heard the sounds of an emergency vehicle. I can describe the motorcycle accident in great detail, including the man's fall, but I can also recall lying in my bed watching the dream. What becomes clear through this kind of dreaming and related manifestations of the dream content is that there are subtler realms of reality transcendent of time and space that play out in the world of matter.

Regarding space in particular, although we are conditioned to think of it as an absolute, we are not bound by it. In our everyday reality, things have very specific locations in space, but in subtler realms of reality, location ceases to exist. A point in space becomes equal to all other points in space, and it is meaningless to speak of anything as separate from anything else—a property physicists call "nonlocality."[1]

In a dream, location is an illusion because everything—people, objects, space, action, and so on—is unfolding out of the more fundamental reality of the dreamer, which is the Dreaming. The pair of hands that protected the woman's head as she tumbled to the pavement manifested out of the more primary, deeper, implicate level of reality and happened to enter her awareness. My consciousness at the time was seemingly in several locations simultaneously—at the accident scene and also in bed watching the dream. On the implicate level of reality, separateness appears as an illusion and all things are ultimately interconnected. There is something about experiencing this primary level of reality that evokes intense joy and love.

The idea that the subtler levels of reality can be accessed through a shift in consciousness alone is a main premise of the yogic tradition. The yoga teacher and mystic Sri Aurobindo once remarked, to discover the "new country within us" we must first learn how "to leave the old one behind."[2] This shift in consciousness, however, can be challenging. The poet Rainer Rilke, feeling curtailed by interpretation, commented, in a letter to a friend, "Wherever an individual's philosophy develops into a system, I experience the almost depressing feeling of a limitation."[3] For me, the more I have silenced my mind and traveled inward, free of interpretive frameworks, the more I have perceived and engaged with subtler levels of reality, beyond space and time, composed of formless vibration. These realms, in turn, were reflected in my dreams.

Since my first dreams, my consciousness had already been expanded. And the further expansion of consciousness I now experienced revealed the separation of consciousness and matter as illusory, allowing my consciousness the freedom to soar into the subtler realms of reality that influence the objective world.

—— *D R E A M I V* ——

Merging with the Dreaming

*A*lthough my strength improved following my first transformative dream experiences, I still had difficulties. After prolonged mental concentration, my consciousness would invariably want to expand without limits. Further, whether my eyes were closed or open, my awareness could be in two or more places at once, which undermined my physical strength and mental balance, and made me cautious about merging entirely with the Dreaming.

At the same time, I had regained normalcy in at least some ways: I was able again to take a lively interest in conversation, and the deep feelings of affection for family and friends that appeared to have dried up two years earlier now stirred in my heart again. The following prophetic dream, which occurred

*in winter 1998 during a snowstorm, began as an ordinary
dream but quickly transformed into a lucid dream and then into
an experience of merging directly into the Dreaming, making
me more aware than ever of the level of reality that is the source
of all creation.*

I dreamed I was driving to work in morning rush-hour
traffic. As I rounded a curve on the highway, I saw a car in
the far left lane spin out of control on the ice, cross three
lanes of traffic, and hit a brown sport utility vehicle (SUV).
The SUV rolled and landed on the side of the road upside
down. I could see a woman's brown hair hanging out the
side window, its glass shattered. I brought my own vehicle
to a sliding stop and parked on the side of the highway.
The first to arrive on the scene, I cautiously walked to the
driver's side of the crashed car and observed that the
woman was unconscious. I then heard another car spinning
out of control and knew it was going to hit me.

At that moment I awakened within the dream, which
now continued in slow motion. I felt the impact of the car,
before it catapulted me twenty yards. When I landed, my
hands and arms were crushed under the vehicle, and I was
unconscious. As I was being loaded into an ambulance,

the EMTs were assessing my apparently comatose state, but I was aware of everything, including their discussion of the woman who had died in the SUV.

After arriving in the emergency room at the local Level I trauma center, I was wheeled into surgery, where a team of doctors placed medical devices on my fingers, hands, and forearms. As I listened to their conversation, the coursing energy in my body began pulsing, which I knew was causing spontaneous healing. I could feel the changes unfolding deep in the bones and tissues of my body. While my awareness merged with this healing energy, I felt rapturous.

Upon first awakening from the dream, I knew I had been shown spontaneous healing, but as I awakened further I could feel the experience fading from my consciousness, along with that knowledge. Two days later, parts of this dream materialized and I became aware of its prophetic nature. I was driving to work in morning rush hour during a snowstorm. At first these details did not trigger uneasiness about a possible materialization of the dream. When traffic slowed and eventually stopped, however, I saw the same accident that was in my dream. This time I was not the first one on the scene, for I was at least thirty cars back.

Still, I could see brown hair hanging out the shattered side window of the upside-down SUV. As emergency vehicles began arriving, I said a prayer for the woman's spirit and suddenly became merged with her awareness. She knew she was dead, and consequently so did I since I was one with her circumstances. Then I felt the now-familiar coursing energy expanding and an extraordinary rapture. But because I couldn't afford to lose the boundary of my own awareness due to the circumstances, I forced myself to pull out of this experience. My awareness separated from hers, and once again I was sitting behind the wheel of my car waiting for the accident to clear.

Later that afternoon I called a good friend of mine who worked in the intensive care unit at the trauma center to inquire about any patients from the car accident that morning. She said they had received one injured patient and there was one dead at the scene. That evening I told her about my dream, describing the emergency room, the medical center, the faces of the doctors I had seen in the dream, and the contraptions that were placed on my hands, which I now know were external fixators. She confirmed all of these details to be correct, even though I had no prior knowledge of the medical center or its personnel.

Another synchronistic event that followed the dream and related to one of its themes was a visit by a woman seeking spontaneous healing. The very next morning, a Lakota friend came to my house unannounced. Over a cup of tea, she said, "I have no idea why, but you are the person who is going to help me spontaneously heal my colostomy." Her words astonished me, for I had not shared the dream events of the previous day with anyone except my friend who worked at the hospital. Upon recovering from my astonishment, I felt resistance and said, "You are mistaken." But she replied, "No, you are the one. Perhaps you will change your mind."

Reflections

As a result of this dream, I had to deal with my increasing capacity for clairvoyance in dreams and its possible significance. The fact that through my dreams I had developed the power of prophecy brought me no elation but instead an uneasiness, since I never knew which of the dream scenes would manifest in real life. By now I had become accustomed to the idea that my dream experiences could be somewhat different from how or when they later materialized. I also knew that the timing of their materialization could also vary. Dreams occasionally materialized within days, sometimes months, sometimes years. Now and then every detail would be correct, while at other times a few would be off, or something would be added. The details about the fatal accident and description of the medical center were correct. Yet, the reenactment of the dream scene fortunately eliminated my own personal tragedy. In this case, I wondered why the actual event differed from the original dream. Perhaps, I thought, the dream had emerged from the implicate level of reality moving toward unfolding in our everyday world, and the act of dreaming had somehow influenced the outcome.

Another new and significant aspect of this dream was the spontaneous healing that seemed to come about in the hospital. During the spontaneous healing part of the dream, I had merged completely into the Dreaming, with no separation between my awareness and the activity of spontaneous healing. When you completely merge into the Dreaming, you are not aware of yourself as an actor apart from the action; you are in a state of experiencing. The vast nature of reality becomes available, and the possible outcomes seem to be limitless, but you have no desire for a certain one.

Consequently, in time I realized that my negative response to my Lakota friend's request for spontaneous healing was wise, since now I sensed that the capabilities emerging in me would have been seriously impeded had I attached importance to a specific outcome implied by the effort to heal others.

This dream also gave me more general insights into my relationship to the Dreaming. In the dream scene when I was in my car and my awareness merged with that of the woman who had been killed, the experience was similar in feeling to the one where my awareness merged with my father's at the time of his death. Both cases involved merging completely into the Dreaming. There was no woman or father, nor was I present; there was only awareness and a feeling of ecstasy. Further, both experiences reminded me of the jaguar dream and the indescribable ecstasy associated with dissolution and limitlessness. As a result of these comparisons, I was beginning to attain an inner, wordless "vocabulary" for comprehending the development of my consciousness.

The difference between a mind limited by the ordinary intellect and a mind merged into the more subtle realms of reality is analogous to the difference between matter in its solid state and matter in its gaseous state. For instance, two stones cannot occupy the same space, but two fragrances can. A stone has weight and mass that limit what it can do; it can move only if it is moved, and then just in a single direction and at a speed limited by the amount of force acting on it. Fragrance, on the other hand, being matter in gaseous form, has certain properties that could be considered miraculous: powers of diffusion and penetration that allow it to spread at phenomenal speeds over great distances in all directions at once, the ability to be in more than one place at a time, and the capacity to pass through barriers and to coexist in the same space with bodies of a similar material. Now I also realized that when you completely merge into the Dreaming, all of these properties and more can be experienced.

Merging completely into the Dreaming expands the self to infinite dimensions, dissolves the sense of separation between ourselves and other people and things, and allows capacities that lie dormant within us to emerge. Rapture accompanies this experience; instead of seeking or knowing love as a desirable end, you *are* love. In this realm, reason releases its power over us.

—— *DREAM V* ——

Materialization and the Challenging of Conventional Reality

*B*y *spring 2000, I was experiencing a progressively expanding field of consciousness and a gradually increasing luminosity of objects, both in the physical environment and in my mind's eye. Whenever the luminosity suddenly intensified, my impulse to merge into it grew stronger, and my awareness would dissolve into limitlessness. Although these events could still challenge my physical strength and mental balance, recovery required less time. With increasing confidence in the stability of my physical and mental processes, I began to travel and work more. The following dream, however, presented me with new challenges regarding the nature of materialization within our conventional reality.*

*A*s my eyes closed, I had the familiar heavy, syrupy sensation that preceded the feeling of energy coursing inside and outside my physical body. When the energy began to surge through me, I awoke within a dream. I was walking through a semiarid, rocky terrain laboring for breath, as if at a high altitude. The sun was beating down mercilessly so I stopped in the shade of a rock ledge. As I was reaching for my water bottle, there suddenly appeared from behind a boulder a small man with closely cropped black hair, dark brown skin, and high cheekbones who looked native with Asian features. He was carrying a jar containing a thick brown liquid. Acknowledging me without looking at me directly, he then sat down six feet away, also taking advantage of the small amount of shade provided by the rocky outcrop. He offered some of the liquid to the earth, said a prayer to the sky, and held up the jar to offer me a drink.

Even before moving to sit next to him, I could smell the pungent, fetid odor of the liquid in the jar, causing me to feel nauseated and altered in some indefinable way. Then when he began speaking to me in a guttural, rhythmic language I had never heard before, I was startled that I understood it perfectly and responded in the same language. The strangeness of the guttural sounds coming from deep in my throat and the nauseating odor of the liquid made me anxious. Eager to end the encounter, I thanked him with a gesture of my head and said in plain English, "I must go now." Standing up, I seemed to be fine, but when I began walking, suddenly my right ankle rolled over, and I plunged down a three-foot rock embankment.

I awakened from the dream holding my right ankle and screaming in pain, the injury having somehow materialized from my dream experience. I jumped out of bed and hopped around on one foot, wincing and feeling strangely altered. By the end of the day, my ankle had swollen to twice its normal size and turned purple and blue, a concrete reminder of an incomprehensible materialization from my dream experience.

The following week I was to lead a ten-day trek in Canyon de Chelly, Arizona, for students training in shamanic lore and practices, a program that included daily hiking, ceremony with the Navajo, and a vision quest. I certainly was not going to cancel the event, so instead I limped through the long hikes. When my Navajo friend and guide asked how I had sprained my ankle and I told him, he chuckled about the way it had happened. Meanwhile, I knew I was going to be in Honduras a month later and worried that this dream might manifest there.

This dream did, in fact, manifest, but not until two years later. I was traveling in Peru with a Peruvian friend named Ernesto. We had arrived in Cusco early in the morning after riding a local bus all night from Puno. We had several hours before needing to catch the train to Machu Picchu, so Ernesto suggested we visit Tamba Machay, "Sacred Temple of the Waters."

After we cleansed ourselves at the temple, Ernesto lay down against a tree and pulled the brim of his hat over his eyes. I knew he had to be tired, since we had been up all night, so I let him sleep while I wandered off to relieve my bladder. I walked down a well-traveled alpaca trail, heading for a rocky outcrop I had spotted around the corner. Turning the corner, I saw a small native man with high cheekbones and Asian-looking eyes, and a jar of brown liquid beside him—the same man and rocky outcrop I had seen in my dream. As in the dream, he acknowledged me without looking at me.

Beginning to slip into the altered state I had experienced in the dream, I knew I had to leave before losing the ability to move. When I turned to go, I found Ernesto standing behind me. He knew the man sitting in the shade of the rock, and they exchanged greetings and conversed for a moment. As I heard the same guttural, rhythmic language that had been in my dream, my head began to reel. I walked briskly down the trail, and when Ernesto caught up to me he told me the man was don Martín, the most renowned sorcerer of the area and a friend of don Manuel Quispe, the Q'ero master shaman with whom I had been working for five years.

Over the next several years I encountered don Martín many times, once spending ten days in ceremony with him and a small group of Westerners who were participating in shamanic training. Eventually, I found out that the sorcerers of Peru, like don Martín, never look anyone in the eye, for the eye is considered the doorway to spirit flight. Subsequently, when I told Ernesto about my dream and its manifestation in Peru, he said, "It probably was not coincidental that you met don Martín in your dream and again on that day. The medicine that comes through you is very much like the sorcery lineage here in the Andes."

Reflections

This dream made me further ponder the phenomenon of dream scenes materializing in real life. The idea of spraining my ankle in a dream and awakening to its immediate physical manifestation, in the form of a sprained ankle, was inconceivable to me at the time. Also discovering that this was yet another prophetic dream, though the event in real life ended differently, left me again apprehensive. Subsequently, each time I had a dream experience about my own life, I began to anticipate that it might manifest. Yet because I had no control over my dream states, there was really nothing for me to do but witness them and try to let go of my apprehensions.

Moreover, not only had the dream experience materialized, but within two weeks of the dream, I had three more experiences of materialization, though of a different sort. Two of these involved manifestations witnessed by other people. Two former clients insisted that I had left sympathetic phone messages for them about traumatic events in their lives: one woman's daughter had been killed in an automobile accident, while the other woman's mother had died of cancer. I had not seen these clients for several years, however, and was not consciously aware of the tragedies, and did not even have the women's phone numbers. The third experience involved a student who claimed she had seen me in two different places nearly simultaneously. She was bewildered to see me teaching, claiming that she had just walked out of my office after meeting with me there. I had been teaching for forty-five minutes, had not left the room, and had not seen her before she entered the classroom.

These three experiences, coupled with the dream, made it clear to me that somehow a part of me was active in imperceptible realms and that this activity had an impact in the manifest world. Combined with my wonderment was anxiety about how to handle such events. I felt as if I had entered some strange new land that defied logic, where mystical forces were the norm.

As a result of this dream experience, my perception of matter and energy changed. I could more readily perceive an internal glow that was always in rapid motion. The millions of tiny cells that made up my flesh and bones I now perceived as a conglomerate of forces whirling together. The more accustomed I became to seeing beyond the world's solidity and to viewing myself as pure awareness, boundless and insubstantial, the more I sensed the formative role of consciousness in creating our reality. Physicist Fred Alan Wolf notes something similar in his book *Taking the Quantum Leap,* when he states that by identifying with the "quantum wholeness" of the world, the observer "becomes" the observed. "He is what he sees."[1]

Further, I began to hypothesize connections between degrees of luminosity and the tendency toward materialization. I sensed that my materializing had something to do with my perception of increasing luminosity of both external and internal objects. Each time the luminosity increased, a realm beyond space and time, composed of infinite vibrations, appeared to unfold. As a result, it seemed possible not only to absorb vast amounts of information at once, like through a telepathic sense of "luminous pictures," but also to exist as a form of pure vibration and reconfigure as energy into another form, as, for example, in experiences of bilocation, when I was lying in bed dreaming and at the same time standing at the foot of another person's bed. Over the years, I have come to recognize when a dream experience is materializing by the degree of luminosity and energy density involved in the reconfiguration of my energy into another form in my dream. But whether I am aware or unaware of materializing, I have no control over it.

I also sensed a connection between my training in shamanism and martial arts and my new awareness of degrees of luminosity. I realized that both shamanism and the martial arts rely heavily on techniques for absorbing energies from nature, and I presumed that the amount of energy taken in by the body determined the degree of luminosity, which in turn dictated the amount of awareness present in a nonlocal experience, some of which might materialize physically. It was my perception that these events of materialization were more likely to happen when my consciousness was expanding and my energy abundant.

Materialization challenges our conventional ideas about reality, since the creation of a person or object out of "thin air" rocks the very foundation of our worldview. Certainly, current scientific understanding is incapable of explaining this phenomenon. Direct experience informing us that the mind is sourced from the implicate order of reality, however, suggests this order of reality gives birth to the physical universe and thus can create all phenomena, including the laws of physics. Viewing levels of reality in this way helps us see that not only is materialization possible but virtually anything is possible. Such events offer a glimpse of the enormous potential that lies dormant in all of us.

—— *D R E A M   V I* ——

Stepping Outside of Time

*B*y now I was experiencing more participatory exchanges
with the forces of nature, as well as more "simultaneous realities," as I call them—two waking realities unfolding at the
same time, although one is not manifest in the physical world.
I was also becoming increasingly aware of the absence of
linear time on other levels of reality.

Participating in a discourse with the animate world had
become second nature to me because of my shamanic training
with the Q'ero medicine people. For example, once while walking on a mountain in Peru, I had listened to stories told through
the voice of the wind, felt the mountain looking at me, and participated in a ceremony where a Q'ero medicine man invited the
lightning to join our activities, resulting in lightning strikes.

The following dream, which occurred in fall 2000, made me aware of how possible it is to relate to nature's energetic forces and how time, as we know it in ordinary reality, does not exist on other levels of reality.

A friend and I were exploring potential locations for a student shamanic training expedition in southern Utah. After two grueling days of hiking into a canyon wearing sixty-pound backpacks in temperatures close to triple digits, we reached the ruin site that was our destination and set up camp along a nearby stream. Just before sunset I told my friend I was going to take a quick look at the ruins, five hundred feet up the cliff, tucked under the rim of the canyon wall, and then we could explore it further the next day.

I left my backpack, taking only my remaining water, and scaled the slip rock to find an Anasazi ruin with an intact kiva, or ceremonial chamber symbolic of the people's origin, including the original ladder descending into it. I climbed down the twelve feet into the kiva, intending to simply sit for a moment in this sacred place. The interior was dark except for a shaft of light penetrating from the opening above. There were shards of pottery and stone implements in the cubicle niches as if they were still holding offerings to the spirit realm. I placed a gift I had brought to honor the ancestors in one of the niches and sat on the ground.

Suddenly I was overcome with sleepiness, and a space-time continuum unlike that of everyday reality opened up. A man, small in stature with jaw-length black hair, was sitting next to me. In addition to seeing him, I could smell his clothes and feel the warmth of his body. Speaking to me in a language I understood perfectly, though it was not one with which I was familiar, he conveyed that this time had already been dreamed and that he wanted to show me something. From previous experiences with simultaneous reality, I knew that if I did not engage with this apparition, it would fade. And I did not want to let it disappear, for I suddenly realized it was probably the significance behind traveling to this remote area of Utah.

As I was thinking this, the man reached out slowly with his left hand. His fingers were spread wide and there was dirt under his nails; it was the soiled, callused hand of a middle-aged man. He then placed his hand on my left shoulder, making me feel like I might pass out from the heaviness of the altered state descending upon me. Immediately I experienced the familiar coursing of energy through my body. As a glow in my head increased in brilliance, an uncontrollable impulse to merge into it grew stronger. Merging, I became a vast sea of light perpetually in motion. Swirling in innumerable currents, both the man and I began evaporating. My awareness then dissolved into the limitlessness of infinity.

After an indefinite period of time, I again became the innumerable currents of light swirling into vortices. I was the vital intelligent medium working as an architect of organic structure. Then as the luminosity slowly decreased, I became aware of energy repatterning in my body and of flesh materializing. My head immediately began to spin, and just when I thought I might pass out, everything steadied.

Following this experience, I wondered if I had just been shown how the Anasazi, a community that once flourished here, left the earth and why there was no evidence of their departure. Although it is not known how or why the Anasazi suddenly disappeared, some Hopi maintain that the Anasazi, having perfected themselves in this life through harmonious interactions with nature and one another, simply ascended to the fifth level of creation.[1] Considering this made the observer within me witness an internal unraveling that left my head swimming. Apparently it was better for me not to engage this question and to let the knowledge remain a mystery.

Night had descended, and I now wondered if I had awakened to the right reality. I saw lightning bolts light up the kiva walls and heard loud claps of thunder and rain beating down. I fell asleep wondering if I would feel the rain, and if, upon feeling it, that would mean I was in the right reality. The thought that I could engage in multiple realities of past, present, and perhaps even the future was daunting to me.

When I awoke and saw daylight, I again wondered if I had awakened to the right reality. How could I be reassured that in climbing down from the slip rock of the ruin site I would return to our campsite and my familiar awareness? Although I had lived through many such circumstances, returning from strange realms of consciousness with my range of awareness redefined, somehow this seemed different, paradoxically filling me with a feeling of both ecstasy and anxiety.

When I arrived back at the campsite, my travel companion was there drying out our belongings over a fire. She handed me a cup of coffee and asked where I had ended up the night before. While sipping hot coffee and appreciating its familiarity, I told her I had stayed in the kiva.

Surprised, my friend replied that when the storm had started, she had come to get me and found my water bottle in the kiva but not me. She had come back down before the rock became too slippery, figuring that once the rain started I would probably stay up there.

My head began to swim considering the possibility that the experience of watching my flesh disappear had meant I had actually dematerialized. I clung to my coffee cup, desperate to feel the ordinariness of this morning following an evening during which I seemed to have stepped outside of time.

Reflections

By the time I returned home from this trip, I had regained mental equilibrium, although I still found it difficult to fully comprehend and process the experience of dematerialization. With the passage of time, I increasingly adjusted to multidimensional consciousness.

Even so, this dream experience was so out of the ordinary that I realized the futility of revealing it to others and so said nothing about it, even to those most intimately connected with me. As a result of the dream, a profound change in my cognitive functioning occurred, as if I had learned a foreign language. I still live in linear time, but it is no longer real to me or fundamental to my nature. Whether this change is due to the experience of completely merging with the Dreaming during the waking dream or the experience of dematerializing and rematerializing, something shifted irrevocably in the crucible of my perception.

After this event, I knew with more clarity that both space and time are by-products of our perception. I knew I had stepped beyond time, beyond death, and then had known the way back to the physical body. I also realized that the source of the body was the same as the source of all things—the Dreaming, a level of reality where the body and mind are not separate, where time and space are non-existent, and where there is no causal connection between events. At this level of reality, there seems to be an infinite number of abstract potentials manifesting simultaneously in the present.

Through this waking dream experience, it was now clear to me that we have multiple ways of exploring the world—listening with our ears, touching with our skin, seeing with our eyes, tasting with our tongue, smelling with our nose—and pathways continually open outward from the perceiving body, engaging with limitless reality. I entertained the ideas that perhaps we are the organs and flesh of the Dreaming, and the Dreaming is perceiving itself through us—or maybe the world is nothing but an objectified dream, and whatever our powerful mind experiences comes to pass because consciousness and matter are one.

—— D R E A M V I I ——

Reconfiguring Energy

In the months following the dream experience in the kiva, the most remarkable feature of my condition was the increased luminosity of both internal and external objects, and this became ever more alluring. The more I allowed myself to merge without resistance into the Dreaming, which happened often, the more difficulty I had operating day to day. I was so overwhelmed by the splendor of the Dreaming that everything of this world—all things conceived by us, every ambition and desire, even my individual existence—appeared banal by comparison.

I was astounded at the incalculable bountifulness I had found within myself. The anxiety and doubts I had entertained about my condition for several years vanished altogether, yielding to a feeling of inexpressible thankfulness. The following dream experience, which occurred in spring 2001, made me increasingly attentive to the reconfiguration of energy as my awareness merged with other objects and people.

I dreamed I was lying on my back under a tree, with my arms beneath my head. Looking up, I noticed a raptor perched in the branches. Initially I thought it was a hawk, but upon closer scrutiny I could see it was an immature bald eagle. As I noted this, it came shooting down at me. I rolled to my right to cover my face, whereupon the eagle buried its beak into my left shoulder blade behind my heart.

As the beak penetrated my body, my consciousness became boundless, expanding immeasurably in all directions. The experience was similar to the first dream I had, in which my consciousness had radically shifted, but in this dream I did not have any of the terror or anxiety previously associated with the limitless extension of my consciousness. On the contrary, I awoke from the dream, affected to the roots of my being by the resplendence of what had just happened. From the nature of the experience, I assumed the encounter with the eagle was a transmission of some kind.

In the days that followed, I could not integrate the magnitude of my expanded consciousness with my everyday world. My emotions became amplified, and my imagination grew highly excitable and vivid. Because of intensified feelings and fatigue due to my inability to sleep, it took everything in my power to maintain emotional stability.

One evening, after three days of no sleep or emotional steadiness, being ecstatic one moment, weeping the next, I went into my meditation room to rest my eyes. Numerous images swirled through my mind until a full figure of Jesus appeared, at which point the other images stopped spinning. While remaining in my own consciousness, I had a dialogue with Jesus. Skeptical, and having little familiarity with him, I asked why he was there.

He said, "To deliver a message."

I asked why him.

He said, "I already delivered a gift. I did it through the eagle so you would be more receptive. I am here to help you integrate a piece of the gift."

I was painfully aware that I was having difficulty integrating the latest expansion in consciousness. Unnerved, I asked him what message he wanted to deliver.

He said, "Embody me and you will know."

I remembered that Swami Muktananda, in his auto-biography, *Play of Consciousness,* discussed embodying his guru.[1] I knew this was related to merging into the Dreaming. I considered merging into the image of Christ before me, but because my mind was already in a precarious state I elected not to do so.

Coming out of this semi-trance state, I assumed I had been receptive to Christ consciousness because Easter was only a few days away.

Reflections

With the benefit of hindsight, I am convinced that if I had embodied Christ that evening I would have learned valuable information about where the boundary between consciousness and matter dissolves. Perhaps I would have been given the key to fluidity in reconfiguring energy to merge with objects and people. Instead, I had to learn the process in an arduous manner.

Consequently, for the next eighteen months I had dream experiences of simultaneous realities, both sleeping and waking, involving merging into various forms. I began merging into almost anything, reconfiguring myself energetically to become those forms—animals, plants, stones, buildings, corporations, and people—even at great distances. I call such dream experiences "reconfiguration dreams." Consistent to all of them were reconfigurations of the energy in and around my body as my awareness became each form, and experiencing the feeling states of those with which I merged. I presume this phase of dreaming was training my consciousness to be more fluid and perhaps awakening the energy of my body.

For example, during this period I was in Peru, making an early-morning ascent to the town of Marcahusi, at 14,000 feet, on a packhorse. I had surrendered to drowsiness and closed my eyes. Within a moment, I was merging with an African American woman who was standing outside her front door, knocking on it, with a bag of groceries in her arms. A man, whom I knew to be her husband, greeted her at the door. As she entered the house, I became her. The energy required to reconfigure and become her, to feel through her, to see through her eyes, was enormous. All of a sudden I was jolted back into ordinary awareness, feeling exhausted after reconfiguring my energy patterns while merging with the woman but otherwise riding along on my horse as if nothing had happened.

Through these dream experiences I underwent significant developments. First, my consciousness was routinely exteriorized, or located outside the limits of my physical body. After the first dream experience, in 1996, my "I," or ego, remained, but instead of being a confining unit, it encompassed a vaster dimension. Now, however, I could perceive an event that included my "I," viewing it from a perspective outside myself. My exteriorized consciousness could engage either physical reality or more subtle realms of reality outside of space and time. Second, my exteriorized consciousness could reconfigure as another form, or reconfigure as that form and then merge into the energy both within and behind that form, or merge into that energy and then begin to reconfigure. Third, my exteriorized consciousness could slow down, speed up, or relocate instantaneously.

Finally, my exteriorized consciousness brought experiences to life even more vividly than when my consciousness was identified with the body. I learned that it is not like remote viewing, in which distant locations are perceived through the power of the mind and no emotions are felt. When consciousness becomes exteriorized, events are more vivid than normal, and you experience the thoughts, feelings, and actions of the form into which you merge. Ken Eagle Feather also alludes to this phenomenon in describing the dream practices of the Toltecs.[2]

It was during these months of reconfiguration dreams that I became aware of entering other people's dreams. I awakened both in the dreams of people I knew and in dreams of strangers—a phenomenon I didn't realize was happening until clients reported dreams with which I was already familiar.

Further, it was through awakening in others' dreams that I realized I had developed exteriorized consciousness and learned how participation with the Dreaming impacts reality and the expansion of consciousness. When I would wake up in someone's dream, it took every ounce of effort to reconfigure into the form in which I was arriving. I discovered I was being taught how to maneuver among energies and shift from form to formlessness within the Dreaming. In the process, I learned that the luminous energy within the Dreaming is force when applied to inorganic matter, and life when applied to the organic plane.

It was also during this time that I noticed my mind

often expanded without encountering barriers and that I was able to influence the subtle forces of nature. I could alter circumstances, change destinies, and modify the effects of other people's actions. I knew transcendent states led to freedom from the physical laws of nature, but I was uncertain about how I wanted to relate to this power.

Eventually, I became paralyzed by my difficulty integrating expanded states of consciousness and the increasing pressure to make my healing capabilities available to others. Consequently, I decided to renounce the everyday world to recover my physical and emotional health. It seemed best, at this point, to simply dissolve into the chaos as the caterpillar melts inside its cocoon before the disintegrated mess is transformed into a butterfly. To gain the time and space necessary to assimilate transcendent reality into my life, I moved to the island of Kauai for an extended period of time.

—— *DREAM VIII* ——

Dominion with Nature

*U*pon my arrival in Hawaii, my consciousness continued to expand. Now such experiences were increasingly becoming a source of strength and happiness. This development had been gradual, and I believed the adjustment was due to the improvement in my general health in the tropical climate rather than to any transformative process in me.

In spring 2003, while attempting to further integrate aspects of my dream experiences, I began work on a manuscript about the Q'ero medicine people's mastery of living in harmony with nature. Soon after, I went to the island of Oahu to visit my brother, a lieutenant colonel in the United States Army, stationed at Pearl Harbor. There, in stark contrast to the people around me, who were fired up by the "War on Terror,"

I was immersed in the art of seeing every moment as sacred.

Thus I became keenly aware of the disparity between the notion of power in America and in the Q'ero tradition, where power is defined by the ability to "push the kawsay," to cocreate with the animating energy of existence—that is, to exercise dominion with all of nature rather than dominance over it. According to the Q'ero, to interact with subtle energies one must learn how to merge the "I" into the energetic field and open the heart. In this state it is possible to effect change with minimal effort and to heal or extinguish life forms with no outward sign of action. For example, when I was hiking in the Andes with a medicine man, we came upon a burro that had broken its leg and was lying on its side, wild-eyed, with maggots crawling out of the open wound. The medicine man stopped and spoke a quick prayer, whereupon the burro relaxed and took its final breath. Acquiring this kind of knowledge and power requires a deep, intimate relationship with all the forces that make up life.

The following dream, which occurred in spring 2003, was my first experience in understanding the power that can come from dominion with, rather than domination over, nature. It also reflects a progression in my exposure to dissolution between the boundary of consciousness and matter, which I

first recognized during the period of reconfiguration dreams.
Such dissolution seems a prerequisite for acquiring the power
that comes from dominion with nature.

I had experienced two nights of repetitive war dreams that
included archetypal themes of torture. During the first
night of dreaming, I was emotionally detached from the
scene, but still had to make decisions to ensure the safety
of everyone involved. The second night of dreaming I
watched myself passively observing repeated scenes of
human misery. Both nights I could not seem to pull out of
the repetitiveness.

The third night of dreaming, because of the familiar
quickening of energy and increase in luminosity in and
around my body, I knew I was going to have a reconfiguration dream. Sometimes such changes in vibration, which
feel as if I am moving with tremendous speed, caused me
to fall out of a dream experience, but now I was able to stay
within it.

As I noticed this, my awareness dropped into a young
woman dressed in a torn military uniform. She had been
beaten, raped, and tortured, her nipples cut off and duct-
taped to her crotch as testicles to degrade her. I could

plainly see the faces of her tormentors and the room with its torture apparatus. I even noted that the duct tape was unlike any with which I was familiar.

As my energy merged with this young woman, I knew her history and could feel that she had dissociated from her body and her spirit was broken. I also felt the familiar sensation of ecstasy that occurs when consciousness is expanding and merging into the Dreaming. As I merged with the woman's mind, the vibration increased to a speed that facilitated moving to another dimension. Then the woman began to pray fervently, yelling, "My Heavenly Father, how great is your mercy. Help me reach the heavens," and I participated in her prayer.

Then as the vibration continued to accelerate and my feeling of ecstasy increased, I simultaneously experienced the woman's feelings of horror and pain, and the torturer's feelings of hatred and rage. Finally, I spun out of the dream.

Upon awakening, the fatigue and internal heat that usually accompanied this kind of dream were not present. I did, however, feel emotionally raw as a result of having simultaneously experienced horrific events and exaltation. The feelings of horror, ecstasy, rage, and disgust stayed with me and increased in intensity whenever I focused on them.

A month earlier I would have stopped this dream experience, separating myself from it, but now something new was happening within my expanding awareness. Every time I wanted to pull out or react, I was shown how to simply be with the experience, mindful of remaining fluid, allowing all these feelings to simply be.

I took the day off from writing, swam in the ocean, and walked on the beach, knowing that with time the emotional residue from the dream would pass. By evening, I still felt vulnerable. As my brother and I were getting ready for dinner, there was an update about the Iraq war on TV— a report about several soldiers from different countries who were being held captive as prisoners of war. Pictures of each soldier were shown. The face of the young woman I had been with the night before in the dream, now a prisoner of war in Iraq, was among them. Touched deeply by the horrific scenes of human misery in my dreaming, I listened in silence.

Reflections

What was unique about this dream experience was that I no longer simply merged into the Dreaming; rather, action was

happening simultaneously through consciousness exteriorized beyond my body and consciousness located in my body.
In this dream experience, I learned how to view that which
is abhorrent and causes heartbreak as part of divinity itself.
The challenge this presented was simultaneously horrific
and glorious. In merging with the woman and her torturer
simultaneously, I came to know love at the source. I entered
the perceptual domain where power is dominion with all of
nature and understood that this kind of power comes
from dominion with the Dreaming that births life itself.

Further, this dream experience was notable for bringing all the elements of transcendent dreaming together for
the first time: coursing energy; reconfiguration of energy
in and around the body, with associated sensation of speed,
increased luminosity, merging into the Dreaming, and the
accompanying feeling of ecstasy; consciousness exteriorized beyond the physical body; and nonlocality. What's
more, once I had merged into the Dreaming, action was
happening *through* me. There was no experiencer or
experience during the dream, only *experiencing*. The result
was action with no actor—behavior free of effort and
personal will, or desire.

After this dream, I became keenly aware of my new-found ability to transcend the boundary that rigidly confines the mental activity of most human beings. I had experienced the dissolution of the boundary between consciousness and matter and yet had not left my body. This was perhaps due to the development of awareness in both the consciousness exteriorized beyond the body and consciousness located in the body, or to the new development of being the experience of multiple forms simultaneously. Regardless, in meeting this young woman and her torturer, my heart had connected with its own source. Through merging directly into the Dreaming, and experiencing it in both my exteriorized consciousness and my body, as if they were one, I experienced the One behind the illusion of separation, and my heart made its home in unity.

This was the integration piece that had been eluding me. Once it fell into place, the most remarkable change occurred—I returned to normal living. Retaining the heightened state of consciousness, I descended from an uncomfortable, unstable state of ecstasy to one of sobriety. My affection for life returned, even greater than before. I once again wanted to love, live, teach, and be in the world. I no longer felt like the caterpillar melting into its cocoon, for I knew I was the butterfly.

—— *DREAM IX* ——

Cocreating with Awareness

*O*ccasionally I returned to Minneapolis for work and struggled increasingly with what to do about knowledge acquired through what seemed to be prophetic dreams. With the ability to step outside of time and influence events or alter destiny comes the need to determine how you wish to relate to these capabilities. In summer 2003, the following dream experience, which involved a client I had been counseling for eight years, made me increasingly aware of my potential responsibility in cocreating events and contributed significantly to how I now choose to relate to transcendent experiences while living in a linear world.

*I*n a dream, I was observing a man sitting behind the wheel of a car suspiciously watching the entrance to a nightclub, as if waiting for someone. It was in Chicago, where I had lived for several years while doing graduate work, and I knew the area in the dream well. Soon the man focused his attention on two women leaving the blues bar and walking toward a parked car—one of whom was a client of mine. My client stopped, said something to her friend, and started walking back toward the blues bar, while her friend remained behind.

The man then got out of his car, came up behind my client, reached under her arm, and held her closely. She evidently knew this man but resisted him. They walked past the blues bar and turned into a desolate alley, arguing loudly. She hit him, and he pushed her so hard she stumbled ten feet and fell to the ground, whereupon he pulled out a gun and shot her. As the shot rang out, I bolted upright in my bed.

That morning, knowing the dream might be prophetic, I contemplated whether I should contact my client and check on her safety. My client was a middle-aged retired accountant a few months short of graduating from a theology program. I had seen her earlier in the week and had supported her decision to get a restraining order against a new boyfriend, a man who had outbursts of anger and poor control of his impulses. Since I had known her for many years, I decided to share the dream with her.

So I phoned and asked if she would be willing to come in for an appointment on short notice. She replied, "I am in Chicago visiting a girlfriend right now." Her response confirmed for me that the dream was likely prophetic, so I told her about it.

Several months passed, during which she missed an appointment and did not answer two phone messages and a letter. Consequently, I presumed she was dead. But a week before my scheduled return to Hawaii, I finally received a call from her. Sobbing and speaking in slurred speech, she requested a consultation for the next day. When she arrived at my office, I was shocked that the formerly vibrant, strong woman was now emaciated, had a facial palsy, a black eye, two broken teeth, and tracks up and down her arms. She told me she had heeded my warning and flown back to Minneapolis, staying with the boyfriend who had followed her to Chicago and helped get her into heroin. In six short months, she was living on the streets as a prostitute and had sought me out because her pimp had raped and beaten her and stolen her money, and she had nowhere to turn.

I offered to take her to the hospital and advocate for her. She shook her head no and asked if I would accept her earring—all she had left—as a gift for the years we had worked together.

I said yes, if she would accept mine in exchange, as a gift to remind her I would assist her. She accepted my earring in return but would not let me help her or tell me where I might reach her.

Reflections

In the days following my encounter with this client, I pondered whether my decision to share the dream had contributed to her suffering. I repeatedly went over in my mind the possible outcome scenarios for sharing or not sharing the dream with her. Had I not told her and had the event happened, maybe she would have been shot but not fatally, motivating her to get out of a dangerous relationship, or maybe she would have recovered only to end up in the same situation anyway. Or perhaps she would have been shot dead and not have had to live another six months on a path of self-destruction. Finally, maybe the dream was only a dream and never would have materialized.

The decision left to me whether to inform my client seemed to result from the fact that in this dream experience I was the observer and did not merge with the Dreaming, so was separate from the action. By comparison, in dream experiences in which I merge into the Dreaming, there is no "I" separate from the action; I am aware of infinite possibilities simultaneously and have no attachment. In such dream experiences, the right action seems to unfold and there is never a decision left to be made in linear time based on personal will.

At last, I was able to clarify my position on how to relate to transcendent reality while living in a linear world, through revisiting chaos theory. Physicists have discovered that many seemingly chaotic phenomena often contain hidden patterns that result in small disturbances causing significant effects over time.[1] They describe this occurrence metaphorically, by saying that a butterfly flapping its wings in Beijing might be the small disturbance that causes a tropical storm in the Caribbean. I wondered, what if our consciousness could intervene at the level of the one butterfly flapping its wings in Beijing in order to prevent the tropical storm in the Caribbean? To do this, we would have to be able to merge with the Dreaming and thus participate in the unfolding of an event.

Again pondering the dream experience about my client, I saw that because I didn't merge with the Dreaming, it wasn't possible to intervene at the level of the butterfly and thus participate in the unfolding of events that affected my client. I was left to contemplate the question, how do you know which butterfly might start a storm in the Caribbean, and in what way is it possible to intervene? Eventually, through more experiences of merging into the Dreaming, I realized that transcendent dreaming is the pathway for experiencing the origin of phenomena. Transcendent dreaming will take you to the Dreaming, and the Dreaming will lead you to the one butterfly that is the origin of the storm and also determine the necessary course of action. Creation and its expression are perfect the way they are.

Since this dream experience, I no longer share dreams that may be prophetic with the subjects within them. Regardless of whether I am an observer in the dream or merged into the Dreaming and a part of the action, my response in linear time is almost always nonaction. In choosing nonaction, I have aligned my own will with the Dreaming, preferring this relationship to power and action. Only in the experience of merging into the Dreaming does one begin to understand that it is not about doing.

Gaining the ability to align and cocreate with the vital, animating energy of creation can only arise from a deep, intimate relationship with the source of life itself. When that source is experienced, the potential inherent within you for dominion with nature and cocreation with the Dreaming is awakened.

DREAM X

Transcendent Living in a Linear World

All together, I lived in Hawaii adjusting to transcendent experiences for three and a half years. During that time, I gained a new vitality and multidimensional reality became organic to my nature. An increasing love for life and humanity were the bloom of frequently merging into the Dreaming. As this affection grew, my desire to reenter the everyday world and serve ultimately led me, in May 2006, to move back to Minneapolis. There I quickly became immersed in the management of transcendent experiences while living in a linear world. The following dream experience, which occurred within six months of my return, made me more aware of the possibility of altering destiny through cocreating with the Dreaming.

I awoke within a dream and found myself at the seashore with a Vietnamese family. While I was witnessing their interactions, the energy within and around my body began to reconfigure, and I merged, one by one, with each member of the family. Every time I merged with another person, I experienced their thoughts and feelings and knew their personal history. This went on all night.

At some point in the dream, when I had returned to observing the family as a whole, I saw a little girl around age six, being pulled under the sea by a riptide. The mother of the child, who had a distinct birthmark on her neck, began screaming in desperation. Bystanders were just observing the child drown. I noted my own indifference to the fact that she was drowning. Then suddenly unable to take the grieving mother's screams anymore, I jumped into the water and saved the little girl. When she was safely on shore with her family, I awoke from the dream. Upon awakening, I was fatigued and irritable from merging repeatedly with different people in the dream and wondered why I had done this with a family from Vietnam.

Interestingly, three nights before having this dream, I had received a call from a nurse practitioner in another state on behalf of a young married couple interested in seeing me for a consultation. When I asked about the nature of the visit, she said they would be more comfortable telling me in person. Since I often choose not to assist a person, I felt it would be better if I knew the nature of the visit before they made the trip, but still I agreed to see the couple.

When they arrived at my office for an evening appointment two days after the dream, I noticed the young woman had a Vietnamese accent. She said she was six weeks pregnant but it was not an opportune time for them to have children, and she wanted me to assist her in a natural miscarriage. Although I had the skill to help in this capacity, I could not imagine why I would want to do this. I informed the couple that I would get back to them within twenty-four hours, and that if I decided to assist them, they would not have to be physically present.

As the woman reached into her purse to hand me her business card, a photograph fell to the floor, rolled about a yard, and landed face up between my feet. When I reached down to pick it up for her, I saw that the woman in the photo had the same birthmark on her neck as the woman in my dream two nights before. Upon closer scrutiny, I could tell it was a photo of the mother in my dream, taken twenty years later.

To make certain the dream experience and the request were related, I asked the young woman if she had had a near-drowning experience as a child. She looked at me with a quizzical expression and confirmed that she had.

After the couple left my office, I picked up the young woman's business card to place it in my briefcase. As I looked at the card, the heavy, syrupy feeling associated with dreaming came over me. I felt the familiar quickening of energy within and around my body, along with the increase in luminosity, and knew I was going to experience a waking dream. I soon found myself in resonance with the energy within the young woman's womb, which first began to disperse, then, as time passed, quieted. I knew that the young woman was having a miscarriage.

The following morning I called the young couple. After the husband answered the phone, I simply said, "I am aware your wife had a miscarriage last night. Please take very good care of her, and please have her call me if she has any questions." I received a card from her a month later thanking me for doing something "I" did not do.

Reflections

This dream emphasized for me how balancing between experiencing the more subtle realms of reality and living in a world that does not acknowledge them is an art. In this dream experience, the fact that my own choice in linear time would most likely have been nonaction did not affect the outcome, and afterward I was left with the responsibility of handling the repercussions in our ordinary world.

Until the linear world evolves to accommodate multidimensional experiences, management of transcendent reality frequently requires soul searching and diplomacy. All the while it must be remembered that walking in balance in the manifest world with the "I" dissolved into the Dreaming is an acquired skill. The thirteenth-century Persian mystic and poet Jalaluddin Rumi expressed such a connection with creation in his poem "This Is How I Would Die" in the line "Come to me naked, there is no one here."[1] Transcendent living feels very much like Rumi's verse.

Another dream experience I had further illuminates the dilemma of diplomatically handling transcendent experiences in everyday reality. Shortly after returning to live in Minneapolis, I decided to see a bodyworker. A friend I respected recommended a practitioner, and when I called to set up an appointment for the next day, the woman suggested I think about an intention for our session. That night before going to bed, I reflected on an intention.

Once asleep, I awoke within a dream sitting at this woman's kitchen table to set the intention for my session with her. We then went into her practice space, where I experienced the entire session. When I awoke a few hours later, I knew the work had already been done since I had the physical sensations that often accompany bodywork. I was faced with the dilemma of how to handle this. I ran through the possibilities. I could simply cancel the appointment. I could cancel the appointment, send her a check, and thank her for the session in the dream. I could go to the appointment, set a new intention, and have a different experience.

Ultimately, I opted to keep the appointment. When I arrived, I encountered the woman from whom I had received bodywork in the dream, as well as the identical kitchen table. I decided to tell her what had happened in my dream, after which I set a different intention for the afternoon's treatment and paid her extra. We had a beautiful session.

Both of these dream experiences exemplify the many capabilities that unfold when transcendent perceptions awaken human potential, including prophecy, clairvoyance, stepping out of time, nonlocality, materialization, and handling the results of such experiences in linear reality. Curiously, almost all individuals who have transcendent capabilities cannot control them at will. This is the beauty of uniting with a force greater than your will.

The Transcendent Human

The dream experiences recounted here are an homage to the intelligence behind and within creation and to the human potential to be awakened in all of us. As I developed increasingly more transcendent capabilities, accompanied by perceptual, physical, biochemical, and energetic shifts, I was continually challenged, physically and mentally, in learning to accommodate my expansion of consciousness and accompanying energy fluctuations, a process still at work in me after seventeen years.

These new capacities included the ability to be in more than one place at a time, to cocreate from imperceptible realms, and to coexist in the same space with bodies of a similar material. Yet the true reward in transcendent dreaming has been merging into the Dreaming and experiencing the universal intelligence behind all forms. When this occurs, the "I" surrenders, and you become one with creation. From such a vantage point, there is only right action that does not come from personal will, desire, or effort; rather, action occurs through you. You learn to live in a noncausal relationship with life. The joy and wonderment so many people are searching for naturally accompany this state of consciousness.

Merging with the Dreaming, however, confounds the mind. Instead of being lost in thinking, you recognize yourself as the awareness behind it. Thinking ceases to be a self-serving, autonomous activity that runs your life. When you are awareness itself, there is no self to engage in thinking. You no longer reflect on the world; you *are* the world. When you are one with the Dreaming, you can return to the true source of your being and participate consciously in the unfolding of that intelligence.

In my contact with transcendent reality I am but a child constantly wondering at what I perceive, trying to decipher a language out of reach of the intellect and more difficult to follow than any I have learned in the manifest world. Indeed, transcendent living is best approached in a spirit of humility, surrendering to the Dreaming that governs creation. Merging into the Dreaming is enrapturing, inspiring, and supremely illuminating because it reveals the sublimity and eternal nature of our being.

Given the chaotic trends evident at present in society,

it seems that the time is near when humankind must relinquish the now worn-out dominant modality of thought and linear time and devise models for achieving transcendent reality. Because our current customs, laws, and values are not designed for a transcendent state of consciousness, the new structures will have to accommodate nonlocal experiences, simultaneous realities, manifestation from imperceptible realms, and other transcendent capabilities. More than likely, our survival in the age to come will depend on our ability to do this.

I have often wondered if, millennia ago at the dawn of reason, the processes of cognitive thought appeared strange to early humans who functioned according to instinctive behaviors. The new faculty of transcendent consciousness, which supersedes reason, may seem just as mystifying.

The growth of human consciousness does not seem to be predictable or linear. It follows a wayward path, advancing in unforeseen leaps, in revelatory epiphanies, one person at a time, often occurring along the margins of contemporary life, like a weed flowering out of a sidewalk crack in a corner of the city. As the heart opens to what lies beyond reason, a new reality emerges and the transcendent human is born.

What undreamed of possibilities will open before us, what extraordinary forces will come under our sway with the further expansion of consciousness, is impossible to fathom at present. The only way to *know* the play of destiny is to surrender to the mystery.

NOTES

INTRODUCTION: *The Dreaming*

1. Coleman Barks, *The Soul of Rumi* (New York: HarperCollins, 2001), 37.

2. John Blofeld, *The Tantric Mysticism of Tibet* (New York: E. P. Dutton, 1970), 61–62.

3. Swami Prabhavananda and Frederick Manchester, trans., *The Upanishads* (Hollywood, CA: Vedanta Press, 1975), 197.

4. Marcel Griaule, *Conversations with Ototemmeli* (London: Oxford University Press, 1965), 108.

5. E. Nandisvara Nayake Thero, "The Dreamtime, Mysticism, and Liberation: Shamanism in Australia," in *Shamanism,* ed. Shirley Nicholson (Wheaton, IL: Theosophical Publishing House, 1987), 226.

6. David Bohm, *Wholeness and the Implicate Order* (London: Routledge & Kegan Paul, 1980), 205.

7. Miguel Ruiz, *The Mastery of Love* (San Rafael, CA: Amber-Allen, 1999), 130.

8. Bernard C. Ruffin, *Padre Pio: The True Story* (Huntington, IN: Our Sunday Visitor Publishing Division, 1982), 263–264.

9. Erlender Haraldsson, *Modern Miracles: An Investigative Report on Psychic Phenomena Associated with Sathya Sai Baba* (New York: Fawcett Columbine, 1987), 26–27.

DREAM I: *A Radical Shift in Consciousness*

1. Gopi Krishna, *Living with Kundalini* (Boston: Shambhala, 1993), 145.

2. David Abram, *The Spell of the Sensuous: Perception and Language in a More-Than-Human World* (New York: Vintage, 1997), 19.

DREAM III: *Piercing the Illusion of Time and Space*

1. Michael Talbot, *The Holographic Universe* (New York: HarperCollins, 1991), 41.

2. Satprem, *Sri Aurobindo or the Adventure of Consciousness* (New York: Institute for Evolutionary Research, 1984), 219.

3. Ulrich Baer, *The Poet's Guide to Life: The Wisdom of Rilke* (New York: Modern Library, 2005), xxxiv.

DREAM V: *Materialization and the Challenging of Conventional Reality*

1. Fred Alan Wolf, *Taking the Quantum Leap: The New Physics for Nonscientists* (New York: HarperCollins 1989), 183.

DREAM VI: *Stepping Outside of Time*

1. Sandra Hinchman, *Southwest's Canyon Country* (Seattle, WA: The Mountaineers, 1990), 23.

DREAM VII: *Reconfiguring Energy*

1. Swami Muktananda, *Play of Consciousness* (New York: SYDA Foundation, 1994), 49.

2. Ken Eagle Feather, *A Toltec Path* (Charlottesville, VA: Hampton Roads, 1995), 194.

DREAM IX: *Cocreating with Awareness*

1. Valerie Hunt, *Infinite Mind: Science of the Human Vibrations of Consciousness* (Malibu, CA: Malibu Publishing, 1996), 53–54.

DREAM X: *Transcendent Living in a Linear World*

1. Coleman Barks, *Voice of Longing* (Boulder, CO: Sounds True, 2002). Audio.

—— SUGGESTED READING ——

Abram, David. *The Spell of the Sensuous: Perception and Language in a More-Than-Human World*. New York: Vintage Books, 1977.

Baba, Meher. *Infinite Intelligence*. North Myrtle Beach, SC: Sheriar, 2005.

Barks, Coleman. *The Soul of Rumi: A New Collection of Ecstatic Poems*. New York: HarperCollins, 2001.

Castaneda, Carlos. *The Art of Dreaming*. New York: HarperCollins, 1993.

Houston, Jean. *Jump Time: Your Future in a World of Radical Change*. Boulder, CO: First Sentient Publications, 2004.

Hunt, Valerie. *Infinite Mind: Science of the Human Vibrations of Consciousness*. Malibu, CA: Malibu Publishing, 1996.

Klein, Jean. *Transmission of the Flame*. St Peter Port, Guernsey, UK: Third Millennium, 1990.

Krishnamurti, J. *This Light in Oneself: True Meditation*. Boston: Shambhala, 1999.

Mindell, Arnold. *Dreaming While Awake: Techniques for 24-Hour Lucid Dreaming.* Charlottesville, VA: Hampton Roads, 2000.

Radha, Swami. *Realities of the Dreaming Mind.* Toronto, Ontario: Timeless Books, 1994.

Ruiz, Miguel. *The Mastery of Love: A Practical Guide to the Art of Relationship.* San Rafael, CA: Amber-Allen, 1999.

Talbot, Michael. *The Holographic Universe.* New York: HarperCollins, 1991.

Wolf, Fred Alan. *The Dreaming Universe: A Mind-Expanding Journey into the Realm Where Psyche and Physics Meet.* New York: Simon & Schuster, 1994.

—— *ABOUT THE AUTHOR* ——

$\mathcal{C}$hristina Donnell, a classically trained clinical psychologist, has studied Eastern traditions and the shamanic energy practices of the Q'ero Indians of Peru for eighteen years. In 1996, she established The Winds of Change Association, an educational organization dedicated to preserving traditions of wisdom that address the education and development of the human spirit.

Christina currently maintains a consultation practice and travels around the world conducting workshop intensives, giving public lectures, and leading experiential expeditions. She lives in Minneapolis, Minnesota.

For further information, please contact:

The Winds of Change Association, Ltd.
1313 Fifth Street SE
Minneapolis, MN 55414
E-mail: windsofchangeLTD@msn.com
Web site: www.wocaassoc.com

ORDER FORM

Quantity   *Amount*

_____ *Transcendent Dreaming:*

    Stepping into Our Human Potential ($12.95) _____

        Tax of 7.15% for Minnesota residents _____

    Shipping and handling ($3.00 for first book;

           $1.00 for each additional book) _____

                Total amount enclosed _____

Quantity discounts available

Method of payment:

❏ Check or money order enclosed (made payable to **Winds of Change Books** in US funds only)

❏ MasterCard   ❏ VISA

_____

Account number   *Expiration date*

Ship to (please print):

NAME _____

ADDRESS _____

CITY/STATE/ZIP _____

PHONE _____

WINDS OF CHANGE BOOKS
1313 Fifth Street SE, Minneapolis, MN 55414
phone: 612-839-6300 • www.transcendentdreaming.com